Anything worth doing
is worth doing slowly.
-Colin Fletcher

Overnight Raisin-Nut Oatmeal

1/4 c. brown sugar, packed
1 T. butter, melted
1/4 t. salt
1/2 t. cinnamon
1 c. quick-cooking oats,
    uncooked

1 c. apple, cored, peeled
    and minced
1/2 c. raisins
1/2 c. chopped nuts
2 c. milk

Place ingredients into a greased slow cooker; mix well. Heat on low setting overnight, about 8 to 9 hours; spoon into bowls to serve. Serves 4.

The first day of school or a Saturday filled with family events usually means a busy morning, so why not make Overnight Raisin-Nut Oatmeal the night before? Putting it together ahead of time means less fuss in the kitchen and a great start to the day!

Cinnamon-Raisin Baked Apples

2 T. raisins
1/4 c. sugar
6 to 8 apples, cored

1-1/2 t. cinnamon
2 T. butter
1/2 c. water

Combine raisins and sugar; spoon into centers of apples. Sprinkle with cinnamon; dot with butter. Place in a 4-quart slow cooker; add water. Heat on low setting for 7 to 9 hours. Makes 6 to 8 servings.

Harvest Apple Butter

4 lbs. apples, cored and
    quartered
1 c. apple cider
2-1/2 c. sugar
1 t. cinnamon

1 t. ground cloves
1/2 t. allspice
4 1/2-pint canning jars and
    lids, sterilized

Place apples and apple cider into a slow cooker; heat on high setting for 10 hours. Sift through a food mill; return pulp to slow cooker, discarding solids. Add remaining ingredients; stir to mix. Heat, uncovered, for one hour; fill sterilized pint jars to within 1/4 inch from the top. Wipe rims and secure lids. Process in a hot water bath for 10 minutes. Makes 4 jars.

A properly working slow cooker uses about as much electricity and resources as a light bulb, making it more economical than using the stove!

Comfy Cider

4 c. apple cider
2 c. cranberry juice
46-oz. can apricot nectar
1 c. orange juice

3/4 c. sugar
2 3-inch cinnamon sticks
1 orange, peeled and
    sectioned

Place ingredients in a slow cooker; heat on low setting until warmed through, 4 to 6 hours. Strain before serving, discarding solids. Serves 10 to 12.

Bring out the slow cooker during an open house or party. Guests will follow the fragrance of a warm drink coming from the crock. Leave beverages on low setting during the gathering and guests can just ladle their drinks right from the cooker.

Mom's Cranberry Tea

3 6-inch cinnamon sticks
30 whole cloves
4 qts. water, divided
16-oz. can cranberry sauce

2 6-oz. cans frozen orange
    juice concentrate, thawed
1 c. sugar
6 T. lemon juice

Combine cinnamon sticks, cloves and 2 cups water in a small
saucepan; bring to a boil and boil for 10 minutes. In a large
bowl, combine cranberry sauce, orange juice, sugar and lemon
juice; add boiling liquid, straining cinnamon sticks and cloves.
Pour mixture and remaining water into a slow cooker; heat on
low setting to keep warm until serving. Makes about 5 quarts.

No peeking! Lifting the lid on the slow cooker allows heat
and moisture to escape and can delay cooking time by
15 to 20 minutes...only remove the lid when stirring
and adding ingredients.

Sizzling Salsa Dip

1 lb. hot Italian ground
    sausage, browned
16-oz. jar hot salsa

16-oz. pkg. pasteurized
    processed mild Mexican
    cheese spread, cubed

Combine ingredients in a slow cooker; heat on low setting until cheese melts, stirring frequently. Makes about 3-1/2 cups.

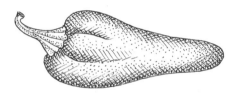

Taco Dip

16-oz. pkg. pasteurized
    processed cheese spread
2 8-oz. pkgs. cream cheese,
    softened

16-oz. jar salsa
1-1/4 oz. pkg. taco
    seasoning mix
1 lb. ground beef, browned

Combine ingredients in a slow cooker; heat on low setting until cheeses melt, stirring frequently. Makes about 3-1/2 cups.

Give extra taste to recipes that use cream cheese by trying one that's flavored...chive, garlic, jalapeo or sun-dried tomato. Yummy!

Quick & Easy Nachos

1 lb. ground beef, browned
1 lb. shredded Cheddar
  cheese
1 T. chili powder
2 t. Worcestershire sauce

14-1/2 oz. can chopped
  tomatoes
3 to 4 jalapeño peppers,
  sliced
16-oz. bag tortilla chips

Combine first 6 ingredients in a slow cooker; stir to blend. Heat on high setting for one hour; reduce heat to low setting and heat for 2 hours, stirring often. Place a layer of tortilla chips on a serving plate; top with beef mixture. Serves 6 to 8.

Look for festive sombreros at party supply stores...line with brightly colored cloth napkins and serve up tortilla chips in style!

Jalapeño-Chicken Chili

2 c. chicken, cooked and
  cubed
4 15-oz. cans Great
  Northern beans
1 onion, chopped
1/2 c. red pepper, diced
1/2 c. green pepper, diced
2 jalapeño peppers, finely
  diced

2 cloves garlic, minced
1-1/2 t. cumin
1/2 t. dried oregano
3/4 t. salt
1/4 c. water
1/2 t. chicken bouillon
  granules
1 to 2 c. salsa

Stir all ingredients except salsa together; spoon into a slow
cooker. Heat on low setting for 8 to 10 hours or on high
setting for 5 hours; stir occasionally. Add salsa during last hour
of heating. Serves 4 to 6.

Start a tradition...slow-cooker
Sunday! Every Sunday
(or whatever day you pick!)
choose a meal to make in the
slow cooker. Just toss all the
ingredients in the crock and
enjoy the day with your family.
They will hardly be able to wait
for dinnertime to roll around!

Grandma's Chili

4 slices bacon, crisply cooked
    and crumbled
1-1/2 lbs. ground beef,
    browned
1 onion, chopped
1/2 c. green pepper, chopped
3 tomatoes, chopped
2 t. sugar

1 t. salt
1 clove garlic, minced
1 T. chili powder
16-oz. can tomato sauce
2 16-oz. cans kidney beans,
    drained
Garnish: sour cream and
    shredded Cheddar cheese

Add ingredients to a slow cooker; heat on low setting for 6 to 8 hours. Spoon into bowls to serve; garnish with sour cream and Cheddar cheese. Serves 4.

Wow them at the next chili cook-off! Serve your
favorite chili recipe with a variety of yummy
toppings...sour cream, chives, shredded cheese, olives
or hot peppers.

Red Bandanna Stew

1 lb. ground beef, browned
2 15-oz. cans new potatoes,
    drained and chopped
8-1/4 oz. can sliced carrots,
    drained

1-1/4 oz. pkg. taco
    seasoning mix
1/2 c. water
Garnish: picante sauce and
    shredded Cheddar cheese

Add first 3 ingredients to a slow cooker; set aside. Combine
taco seasoning mix with water; pour into slow cooker. Heat on
high setting for 30 minutes to one hour; spoon into bowls to
serve. Add a spoonful picante sauce and sprinkle with cheese
to taste before serving. Serves 4.

Beefy Taco Soup

1 lb. ground beef, browned
15-oz. can stewed tomatoes
15-oz. can kidney beans,
    drained and rinsed

1-1/4 oz. pkg. taco
    seasoning mix
8-oz. can tomato sauce

Stir ingredients together; pour into a slow cooker. Heat on
low setting for 6 to 8 hours; stir occasionally. Spoon into bowls
to serve. Makes 4 to 6 servings.

Soups are ideal for casual get-togethers.
Borrow 3 or 4 slow cookers and fill each with a
different soup, stew or chili. Or, better yet, ask
friends to bring their favorite soup to share!

Goulash

2 lbs. stew beef, cubed
1/4 c. oil
2 28-oz. cans potatoes,
    drained and rinsed
4 carrots, peeled and sliced
1 t. dried marjoram
8-oz. can tomato sauce

3 c. water
1 clove garlic, minced
1/2 t. salt
1 t. lemon zest
2 cubes beef bouillon
1 T. paprika

Brown beef in oil in a large skillet; remove from heat and set aside. Combine remaining ingredients in a 5-quart slow cooker; stir in beef. Heat on high setting for 4 hours or on low setting for 7 hours. Makes 4 to 5 servings.

Hollow out a round loaf of pumpernickel bread to serve your soups and stews in...a quick and savory meal the whole family will love.

Easy Potato Soup

4 to 5 potatoes, peeled and
   cubed
10-3/4 oz. can cream of
   celery soup
10-3/4 oz. can cream of
   chicken soup

milk
7.6-oz. pkg. instant mashed
   potato flakes
Garnish: bacon bits, sour
   cream, green onions and
   shredded Cheddar cheese

Place potatoes, soups and one soup can full of water into a
slow cooker; heat on high setting until potatoes are tender,
about 2 to 3 hours. Add one soup can full of milk and enough
instant mashed potatoes to reach desired consistency, stirring
constantly. Heat 2 to 3 hours longer; spoon into bowls to
serve. Top with garnishes. Serves 4 to 6.

The prettiest croutons...cut bread with a small cookie
cutter. Brush cut-outs with butter, place on a baking
sheet and bake at 350 degrees until golden.

Smoked Sausage Stew

4 to 5 potatoes, peeled and
   cubed
2 16-oz. cans green beans
1-lb. pkg. smoked sausage,
   sliced

1 onion, chopped
2 T. butter

Layer potatoes, green beans, sausage and onion in a slow
cooker; dot with butter. Heat on low setting for 4 to 5 hours.
Makes 4 servings.

Fresh vegetables like potatoes, carrots and onions
should be placed in the bottom and along the sides of a
slow cooker, with the meat on top, as they generally
take longer to cook.

Easy Cheesy Potatoes

32-oz. pkg. frozen
    hashbrowns, partially
    thawed
1-lb. pkg. Kielbasa, chopped

1 onion, diced
10-3/4 oz. can cheese soup
milk

Place first 4 ingredients in a 6-quart slow cooker; add one soup can of milk, stirring to mix. Heat on high setting for 3 hours or on low setting for 8 to 10 hours. Serves 4.

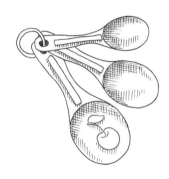

Mom's Baked Potato Salad

5 lbs. potatoes, peeled, cubed
    and boiled
1/2 c. butter, melted
4 c. shredded sharp Cheddar
    cheese

2 c. sour cream
3-1/4 oz. jar bacon bits
salt and pepper to taste

Combine potatoes and butter in a large bowl; add cheese, sour cream and bacon bits, mixing thoroughly. Salt and pepper to taste. Spoon mixture into a slow cooker; heat on high setting for one hour or on low setting for 2 hours, stirring every 30 minutes. Serves 8 to 10.

4-Bean Bake

1/2 lb. ground beef
1 onion, chopped
1 lb. bacon, crisply cooked
    and crumbled
1/2 c. brown sugar, packed
1/2 c. sugar
1/4 c. catsup
1/4 c. barbecue sauce
2 t. mustard
2 t. molasses
1/2 t. chili powder

1 t. pepper
1/2 t. salt
16-oz. can butter beans,
    drained
16-oz. can kidney beans,
    drained
31-oz. can pork & beans,
    drained
16-oz. can Great Northern
    beans, drained

Brown beef and onion in a large skillet; drain. Combine with all
ingredients in a 6-quart slow cooker. Heat on high setting for
one hour; reduce setting to low and heat for 3 additional hours.
Makes 12 to 15 servings.

When toting a slow-cooker dish to a potluck, wrap a
rubber band around one handle, bring it up over the lid
and secure it over the other handle...the lid stays on
nice and tight!

BBQ Slow-Cooker Chicken

4 boneless, skinless chicken
    breasts
3/4 c. chicken broth

1 c. barbecue sauce
1 sweet onion, sliced
salt and pepper to taste

Place ingredients in a slow cooker; stir gently. Heat on
high setting for 3 hours or on low setting for 6 to 7 hours.
Makes 4 servings.

Shredded Beef BBQ

2-lb. beef roast
1 onion, sliced
1/2 c. water
1/2 c. plus 1 T. brown sugar,
    packed and divided
1 T. vinegar

2 t. lemon juice
7-oz. bottle catsup
1/4 t. salt
1-1/2 t. Worcestershire sauce
1/2 t. mustard
pepper to taste

Place roast in a slow cooker; add enough water to cover. Top
with onion; heat on low setting overnight, about 8 hours.
Shred roast with 2 forks; place in a 10" skillet. Add 1/2 cup
water; bring to a boil. Stir in 1/2 cup brown sugar; heat until
liquid evaporates. Combine remaining ingredients with
remaining brown sugar in a mixing bowl; pour over beef
mixture. Heat until warmed through. Serves 6.

*Be sure to unplug and cool the slow cooker completely
before adding water for cleaning...otherwise the
crockery or stoneware liner could crack.*

Pepperoncini-Beef Sandwiches

3-lb. beef roast
1-1/2 c. water
16-oz. jar pepperoncini
   peppers

36 mini croissants
8-oz. pkg. shredded
   mozzarella cheese

Place beef and water in a slow cooker; heat overnight on low setting. Shred beef and add pepperoncinis with juice; heat on low setting an additional 4 to 6 hours. When ready to serve, top each croissant with beef mixture and sprinkle cheese over beef. Makes 3 dozen.

Enjoy the benefits of slow cooking by using
less-expensive (and less-tender) cuts of beef.
The long heating process produces fork-tender,
flavorful beef every time!

Tried & True Meat Loaf

1-1/2 lbs. ground beef	3/4 c. bread crumbs
2 eggs	1/4 c. catsup
3/4 c. milk	2 T. brown sugar, packed
1 onion, chopped	1 t. dry mustard
1 t. salt	1/4 t. nutmeg
1/4 t. pepper	

Combine beef, eggs, milk, onion, salt, pepper and bread
crumbs; form mixture into a loaf. Place in a slow cooker; heat
on low setting 5 to 6 hours. Whisk remaining ingredients
together; pour over beef. Heat on high setting an additional
15 minutes. Serves 4 to 6.

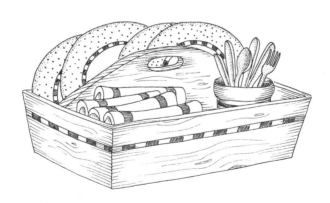

Because slow cookers can sometimes dilute seasonings
over a long period of time, flavorful ground herbs and
spices are best added near the end of cooking.

Creamy Beef Stroganoff

1-1/2 lbs. stew beef, cubed
1 onion, sliced
2 10-3/4 oz. cans cream of
   mushroom soup
2 T. catsup

2 t. Worcestershire sauce
1 t. pepper
1 to 2 c. sour cream
12-oz. pkg. medium egg
   noodles, cooked

Place beef and onion in a slow cooker; set aside. Combine
soup, catsup, Worcestershire sauce and pepper together; stir
into slow cooker. Heat on low setting for 8 to 10 hours; stir in
sour cream and heat through. Spoon over noodles to serve.
Makes 4 to 6 servings.

Spinach Rolls

1 lb. ground beef
3 slices bread, toasted and
   crumbled
2 onions, chopped
1 egg
1 t. salt

1/4 t. pepper
1/2 t. dried marjoram
1/8 t. nutmeg
16 to 20 spinach leaves
1 c. beef broth
2 T. butter

Combine first 8 ingredients; set aside. Boil spinach leaves for
2 to 3 minutes; drain. Place one heaping tablespoon beef
mixture on each spinach leaf. Fold ends together toward
center; roll tightly. Place in a slow cooker; add broth. Dot with
butter; heat on low setting for 6 to 8 hours, adding additional
broth if necessary. Serves 4 to 6.

Scalloped Potatoes & Ham

2 to 3 lbs. potatoes, peeled,
    sliced and divided
12-oz. pkg. cooked ham,
    cubed and divided
1 onion, sliced and divided

2 c. shredded Cheddar
    cheese, divided
10-3/4 oz. can cream of
    celery soup

Layer 1/3 each of the potatoes, ham, onion and cheese in a
well-greased slow cooker; repeat twice. Spread soup on top;
heat on low setting for 7 to 8 hours, stirring occasionally.
Serves 4 to 6.

As your dish nears the end of its cooking time, check on
the amount of liquid in the crock...if there seems to be
too much, remove the lid and cook on high allowing some
water to cook out. If you'd like to thicken the sauce,
stir in cream, sour cream or shredded cheese.

Chicken & Green Bean Bake

2 to 3 boneless, skinless
    chicken breasts
salt, pepper and garlic
    powder to taste
10-3/4 oz. can cream of
    mushroom soup

1/2 c. milk
14-1/2 oz. can green beans,
    drained
2.8-oz. can French fried
    onions

Place chicken breasts in a slow cooker; season with salt, pepper and garlic powder. Heat until juices run clear when chicken is pierced with a fork, approximately 2 to 3 hours on high setting; drain. Add mushroom soup, milk, and green beans; sprinkle top with French fried onions; cover and heat 30 minutes longer. Serves 4.

Family always on the go? If everyone can't sit down together for dinner, the slow cooker can still provide warm meals for all. With the low, slow heating it's unlikely foods will overcook, so you can keep the main dish warm all evening until everyone gets their share!

That's Amore Chicken Cacciatore

6 boneless, skinless chicken
   breasts
28-oz. jar spaghetti sauce

2 green peppers, chopped
1 onion, minced
2 T. minced garlic

Place chicken in a slow cooker; top with remaining ingredients. Heat on low setting for 7 to 9 hours. Serves 6.

Mom's Spaghetti Sauce

1 onion, diced
3 cloves garlic, chopped
1 T. butter
3 14-1/2 oz. cans tomatoes
3 6-oz. cans tomato paste
2 c. water
1/4 t. salt
1/2 t. pepper
1/2 t. dried basil

1/2 t. dried oregano
1/2 t. garlic powder
1/2 t. dried thyme
1 t. Italian seasoning
2 bay leaves
1 T. dried parsley
1/8 t. sugar
3 T. olive oil

Sauté onion and garlic in butter; set aside. Blend tomatoes and tomato paste in a blender until smooth; stir in onion and garlic. Pour into a slow cooker; mix in remaining ingredients. Heat on high setting for approximately 3 hours, stirring occasionally; remove bay leaves before serving. Makes about 5 cups.

Baking soda can bring out the natural sweetness of tomato-based sauce by reducing the acid. Add about 1/4 teaspoon per quart of sauce as it simmers in the slow cooker.

Italian Beef Sandwiches

3 to 4-lb. beef chuck roast,
    trimmed
1-oz. pkg. Italian salad
    dressing mix
2 t. Italian seasoning
8-oz. jar pepperoncini
    peppers

10-1/2 oz. can beef broth
pepper and garlic powder
    to taste
6 to 8 Kaiser rolls, toasted

Combine all ingredients, except rolls, in a slow cooker; heat on low setting 6 to 8 hours. Remove roast, shred and return to slow cooker until warmed through. Spoon onto toasted rolls to serve, using juice for dipping. Makes 6 to 8 servings.

Slow cooking keeps the moisture inside, causing condensation to form on the lid. To avoid spilling into the crock, always lift the lid straight up, rather than tilting, when stirring or adding ingredients.

Slow-Cooker Pepper Steak

1-1/2 to 2 lbs. round steak
2 t. oil
1/4 c. soy sauce
1 c. onion, chopped
1 clove garlic, minced
1 t. sugar
1/2 t. salt

1/4 t. pepper
1/4 t. ground ginger
16-oz. can chopped tomatoes
2 green peppers, sliced
1/2 c. cold water
1 T. cornstarch

Cut beef into 3"x1" strips; brown in oil in a 10" skillet. Transfer to a slow cooker; set aside. Combine next 7 ingredients; pour over beef strips. Heat on low setting until beef is tender, 5 to 6 hours. Add tomatoes and green peppers; heat one more hour. Whisk water and cornstarch together; stir into slow cooker. Increase heat to high setting; heat until thickened. Makes 6 to 8 servings.

To get the most mouth-watering meals when cooking in a slow cooker, be sure ingredients fill the crock at least 1/2 full and no more than 2/3 full.

Landslide French Dip

3-lb. rump roast
1 cube beef bouillon
3 to 4 peppercorns

1/2 c. soy sauce
1 bay leaf
1 t. garlic powder

Place roast in a slow cooker; add remaining ingredients. Pour in enough water to cover the roast; heat on low setting for 10 hours. Remove and discard bay leaf before serving. Serves 6.

Smothered Steak

1/3 c. all-purpose flour
1 t. garlic salt
1/2 t. pepper
1-1/2 lbs. round steak, cut into strips
1 onion, sliced
2 green peppers, sliced

4-oz. can sliced mushrooms, drained
10-oz. pkg. frozen French-style green beans
1/4 c. soy sauce
9 c. prepared white rice

Add first 3 ingredients to a one-gallon plastic zipping bag; shake to mix. Place steak strips in bag; shake to coat. Arrange steak in a slow cooker; layer onion, green peppers, mushrooms and green beans on top. Pour soy sauce over top; heat on high setting for one hour. Reduce heat to low setting and heat for 8 hours; serve over a bed of warm rice. Serves 6.

For easy clean-up, spray the inside of the slow cooker with non-stick vegetable spray before adding ingredients.

Hometown Chicken & Rice

1-1/2 c. long-cooking rice,
    uncooked
parsley to taste
pepper to taste
2 lbs. boneless, skinless
    chicken breasts, cut into
    strips

1.8-oz. pkg. cream of
    broccoli soup mix
2 to 3 c. chicken broth

Place rice in a greased slow cooker; sprinkle with parsley and pepper. Top with chicken; set aside. Combine soup mix and 2 cups broth; pour over chicken. Heat on low setting for 6 to 8 hours, adding more broth if necessary. Serves 6.

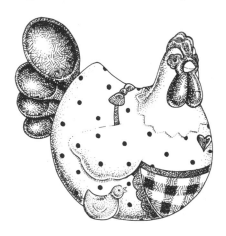

What a time saver! Many cooks use large-capacity slow cookers to cook only once for dinner and have enough left over to freeze for another meal. Just divide leftovers into small portions (in freezer-proof containers) and cool quickly in the refrigerator before freezing.

Slow-Cooker Turkey & Dressing

8-oz. pkg. stuffing mix
1/2 c. hot water
2 T. butter
1 onion, chopped
1/2 c. celery, chopped
1/4 c. sweetened, dried
   cranberries

3-lb. boneless turkey breast
1/4 t. dried basil
1/2 t. salt
1/2 t. pepper

Coat a 4-quart slow cooker with non-stick vegetable spray;
spoon in stuffing mix. Add water, butter, onion, celery and
cranberries; mix well. Sprinkle turkey breast with basil, salt
and pepper; place on top of stuffing mixture. Heat on low
setting for 6 to 7 hours; remove turkey, slice and set aside.
Gently stir the stuffing mixture; allow to sit for 5 minutes.
Transfer stuffing to a platter; top with sliced turkey. Makes
4 to 6 servings.

Have frozen leftovers from a previous slow-cooked
dinner? Be sure to reheat with the conventional
oven...the slow cooking process is not safe for
reheating frozen foods.

★ Classics ★

Cherry Cobbler Dessert

2 21-oz. cans cherry pie
    filling
18-1/2 oz. pkg. yellow cake
    mix

1/4 c. butter, softened
1/2 c. chopped nuts
Garnish: ice cream or
    whipped topping

Spread pie filling in the bottom of a 5-quart slow cooker; set aside. Combine cake mix and butter until coarse crumbs form; sprinkle over pie filling. Layer with nuts; heat on low setting for 3 hours. Serve warm with ice cream or whipped topping. Serves 6 to 8.

Chocolotta Goodness

18-1/2 oz. pkg. chocolate
    cake mix
2 c. sour cream
3-1/2 oz. pkg. instant
    chocolate pudding mix

6-oz. pkg. chocolate chips
3/4 c. oil
4 eggs
1 c. water

Combine ingredients in a large bowl; mix well. Pour into a greased 5-quart slow cooker. Heat on low setting for 6 to 8 hours; do not remove lid during cooking. Serves 6 to 8.

A slow cooker makes a delightful (and welcome) housewarming or bridal shower gift...be sure to tie on a few favorite recipes before giving.

Ooey-Gooey Fondue-y

14-oz. can sweetened
    condensed milk
6-oz. pkg. butterscotch chips
4 1-oz. sqs. unsweetened
    baking chocolate

7-oz. jar marshmallow creme
1/2 c. milk
1 t. vanilla extract

Combine ingredients in a double boiler; heat over low heat until melted and smooth, stirring often. Pour into a fondue pot or slow cooker; keep warm over low heat. Makes 3-1/2 cups.

Melon balls, frozen berries and pineapple chunks make yummy fruit kabobs. Try 'em with Ooey-Gooey Fondue-y...keep plenty of napkins on hand!

Tick, Tock, put it in the Crock!

Many of your favorite recipes can easily be adapted to the slow cooker...just follow these simple guidelines:

★ Ground beef should be cooked and drained before using in a slow-cooker recipe.

★ For best color and flavor, slightly brown chicken in oil before adding to the crock.

★ As a general rule, cut liquid amounts in half when adjusting to the slow cooker.

Follow this time guide when converting recipes:

Conventional Recipe	High	Low
15 to 30 minutes	1-1/2 to 2-1/2 hours	4 to 8 hours
35 to 45 minutes	3 to 4 hours	6 to 10 hours
50 minutes to 3 hours	4 to 6 hours	8 to 16 hours

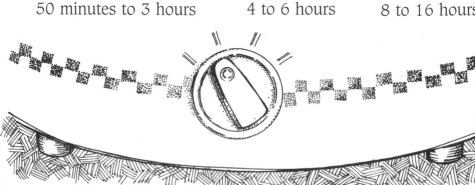

Hey good Lookin'! what's cookin'!

On the MENU...

Cook time: _____ to _____

temperature setting: _____

YUM

Copy and cut out this clever table tent. Fold it in half and jot down the recipe name...set it next to the slow cooker so everyone will know just what's inside and when it'll be ready!

INDEX